…One of the questions a panel of men answered was:

What is it about bottoms?

The men responded to the question for about ten minutes! They described all the different kinds of bottoms there are. They said, "Well, you know, there are firm bottoms and jiggley bottoms and wide bottoms and flat bottoms, and bottoms with more bottom on the top than on the bottom."

I'd never noticed there were so many kinds of bottoms. And I was wondering: *What kind of bottom do I have?* Because you never really know what it looks like back there, right?

Then the oldest of the men summed it up. He said: "What it comes down to is this: no matter the shape of your bottom, some guy is diggin' on it!"

✳ ✳ ✳

"Alison Armstrong's wisdom on relating to men is so pure, so smart, and brimming with so many "ah-ha's" that it's no wonder why nearly everyone I know hangs on her every word... especially me!"

–Linda Sivertsen
Author of *Generation Green* and West Coast Editor of *Balance* Magazine

"This quick read will intrigue women who are open to producing a different result in their relationships with the men in their lives—and are willing take a leap of faith; using science, humor, and acceptance as their jumping off point. Thank you, Alison!"

–David Salinger
VP Programming & Creative, ABC 7 / KGO-TV
San Francisco, Oakland, San Jose

Other Titles
by
Alison A. Armstrong

Keys to the Kingdom

The Amazing Development of Men

In Sync with the Opposite Sex

*Understanding Women:
Unlock the Mystery*

*The Belated Education
of Adam and Eve*

Making Sense of Men

of Men

*A Woman's Guide to a Lifetime of Love,
Care and Attention from All Men*

❋ ❋ ❋

Alison A. Armstrong

Making Sense of Men

*A Woman's Guide to a Lifetime of Love,
Care and Attention from All Men*

For Information:
PAX Programs Incorporated
P.O. Box 56749
Sherman Oaks, CA 91413

UnderstandMen.com

Interior and Cover design: Bette Cowles-Friedlander
CowlesGraphicDesign.com
Cover illustration: Roxana Villa
Roxanavilla.com

ISBN: ISBN 978-1-60530-909-5

First Edition Published 2008
10 9 8 7 6 5 4 3 2

Printed in the United States of America

Contents

※

Acknowledgments

My thanks to the special people who made this book possible:

To Trev for being extraordinary as "the man on the post." Your love, care and attention for me and for PAX gives me the freedom to express the best part of myself in my work. To Leslie for being my partner and my friend. Your love, support and endlessly fascinating ability to build the "dock" makes our mission more than a pipe dream.

To the staff of PAX—Janice, Patrice, Sue, Cathy, Heather and Customer Care—for the love and attention you give to me and to the courageous men and women who are our customers. You are the heart of PAX. To the Workshop Leaders—Donna, Jaime, Kathryn, Leslie, Gilda and Paulette—for joining me long ago in the inquiry, and sharing my passion for "getting the word out" about how great men are. You are the spirit of PAX. To the Workshop Leader Candidates for being the future. Your passion gives PAX the capacity to touch the lives of women who want to celebrate men worldwide.

To Linda Sivertsen for making me a better writer, again. To Penny Phillips for your generous feedback. To Bette and Michael Friedlander for bringing beauty and clarity to our work. To Roxana Villa for once again capturing my vision in your art.

To Greg, the love of my life. It's all possible because of you. To Jeff, Claire and Annie for being a constant source of love, inspiration and laughter. I am so glad you chose me to be your mom. To Mercer, Gabe and Barbara for your priceless friendship.

To all the men and women who have shared this great adventure since 1991. You are my teachers.

✳ ✳ ✳

Introduction

✳

The material contained in this book was originally taught in one of our most advanced programs: Celebrating Men & Marriage™. It cleared up the confusion about how men choose the women they pursue for romantic relationships, while others remained friends or merely bed-mates.

For the women participating in the workshop, it illuminated their pasts, healed old wounds, and gave them a more informed and intelligent way to interact with men in their futures. It made such a difference that it seemed a shame that only those women received it. So I made the decision to make the material available in a live introductory seminar, for women who were considering our curriculum as a possibility for their adult education and transformation.

You can imagine what happened next. The material made such a difference for the thousands of women who came to the live Making Sense of Men seminar, that it seemed a shame that the information wasn't available to women worldwide.

So now it is. And what's even better? Since I'm not limited to a three hour seminar, I can throw in all the juicy tidbits that come to mind. You'll find them in the shaded "side bars." Enjoy!

Alison Armstrong
December 2007

Dedicated to

The Men of PAX

✳ ✳ ✳

We couldn't do it
without your constant love,
care and attention

CHAPTER ONE

Who is to Blame?

✳

There is a good chance, since you're reading this, that you want to make some sense of men and their behavior. You might be frustrated by men. You might be confused by men. You might just want to know how to make relationships with these creatures better. You might want to find a way to get and hold a man's love and attention; a way that could last a lifetime. I did.

Little did I know, when I began my journey, that not only would I learn to make sense of men, I'd also learn the secrets to bringing out the best in ALL men.

I grew up in a pretty traditional family where my father worked and my mother stayed home and I played with Barbie and Ken dolls. It felt perfect. Until the day I came home from elementary school, and my mother was dancing around the kitchen, singing, "Anything You Can Do, I Can Do Better" from the musical *Annie Get Your Gun*. She sang with such energy and defiance that it made a distinct impression. There was this message for me: *Barbie has Ken but Barbie doesn't need Ken! Barbie's better than Ken!*

> **Barbie has Ken but Barbie doesn't need Ken! Barbie's better than Ken!**

From then on, I embraced a new way of being in life: I was going to prove that I was better than my two brothers; I was going to prove that I was better than any man. I was going to make that song come true. I actually did a really good job of it. Maybe you have, too.

> **I wanted the husband and the family and the white picket fence.**

But I still had the dream. I wanted the husband and the family and the white picket fence. So I got married when I was twenty-three years-old to Mr. Tall-Dark-and-Handsome. His name was David and I was smitten with his good looks and intelligence. I wanted those qualities and his naturally slender physique for my children.

Our relationship was a struggle. We weren't close. We weren't intimate. We weren't good friends. I tried everything I could think of to have him love me more, and want to spend more time with me. I even learned how to climb mountains in the snow to improve our relationship.

By the time I asked David for a divorce (when I was almost 30), I was convinced that I just wasn't the type of woman that men really loved. I wasn't the kind of woman that inspired presents or wild passionate lovemaking or romance—or even interest in my life. For whatever reason, I wasn't that type of woman. I concluded (and this dates me) that I just didn't have the Princess Grace gene. I blamed myself for failing to be attractive enough to my husband to inspire what I needed from him.

Pretty soon after leaving my husband (honestly, immediately, as I was absolutely starving for attention), I started a relationship

> **I just didn't have the Princess Grace gene.**

with a man who did all those things that my husband never did. Brian was romantic and attentive and interested in me and my work. It was fabulous. That was the year the movie *Pretty Woman* came out, and it was the first time in almost a decade that I went to a romantic comedy and didn't cry for myself. I watched this romance and thought, *That's happening to me! He's taking me to San Francisco next weekend! Oh, my God! That's happening!*

I was so excited. *There's nothing wrong with me! I do have the Grace Kelly gene!*

Now I was blaming my ex-husband. First I blamed me — now I was blaming him. Everything that was wrong in our marriage was because of him, not because of me! I decided then that I'd simply married the wrong man.

About three months later, I heard myself complaining to my new boyfriend. I was upset about the *exact* same things that I'd been upset about with my husband. He was no longer interested. He was no longer romantic. He was no longer attentive. He was no longer any of the things that I was so excited about before.

> **How did that happen? Why did he change? When did he change?**

How did that happen? Why did he change? When did he change? I

> *Now you know my state of mind when I heard the words that changed my life.*

had to figure it out. I had to figure it out so I could keep it from happening again. Sound familiar? And then I connected the dots. He changed when he caught me. I'd heard that men love the chase, but I didn't know what it meant until now. All the pursuit, all the wooing, all the everything lasted until I was feeling, *Okay, I'm yours.* Then all the good stuff came to an abrupt halt, and he turned into somebody else.

I realized that my ex-husband changed after he'd caught me, too. Oh, and the guy before him—he'd changed. They'd all changed. I thought, *Oh, that's who men are. Men are just con artists on good behavior until they catch you!*

My new love strategy was born. I decided the only way to do this was to pretend I wasn't caught even when I was. That's right—never let them know they've caught you. Now you know my state of mind when, on a fateful Tuesday night in February of 1991, I heard the words that changed my life.

This is what happened: I went to a class with a friend of mine. Her name is Lisa, and we shared a similar view of men—only Lisa was much more vocal than I. Our teacher, Herb, was talking about relationships and love and intimacy and communication. Lisa raised her hand, Herb called on her and she said, "What I want to know is why are men wonderful in the beginning? They'll give you wonderful presents, and they'll take you to romantic places, and they'll listen to you talk about your pets and your family. And then after a few weeks or a few months they turn into sports-watching, pizza-eating, beer-belching couch slugs! Why is that?"

I was watching Herb, because I expected him to get defensive. But he looked like he welcomed the question. He walked up to her slowly and said, "Oh, I see… You're a frog farmer."

I could hear gasps from women around the room. Lisa said, "Huh?" Herb repeated, "You're a frog farmer." She looked at him suspiciously for awhile. With her hand on her hip, she finally challenged him, "All right, all right. What's a frog farmer?" Herb answered slowly, "Some women turn frogs into princes. You, my dear, turn princes into frogs." There was another gasp throughout the room. He turned around, and Lisa stuck her tongue out at him.

The remark didn't connect with Lisa—maybe because it missed her and struck me through the heart. I couldn't move. I sat there thinking… *Uh, I'm a frog farmer. I'm a frog farmer. Uh, oh. I'm a frog farmer.* I had a vision of a big white farmhouse—I'm standing on the porch, and there are rows and rows and rows of frogs with little human heads. My ex-husband was right in the front row, and I realized, *I'm a very successful frog farmer.*

What if there's something I'm doing that is bringing the worst out in men?

I thought of all the men I'd known: Mr. Wonderful, Mr. Perfect, Mr. Right and so on, and how they'd all changed. *What if I have something to do with this? What if there's something I'm doing that is bringing the worst out in men?*

To some people that would be really bad news; to find out it was them all along. But I was jumping up and down. I was excited because if it was me, I could do something about it. If it was me, I could stop. If it was me, I could change it. If I was the one who was turning princes into frogs, then if I changed, maybe they wouldn't.

That immediately presented a problem: I didn't know how I turned princes into frogs. I didn't know what I was doing that was bringing out the worst in men. I could see the result, but I couldn't see what caused it.

I decided to find out by studying men. I decided to learn what brings out the worst in men, so I could stop bringing out the frog. And I had this little glimmer of hope, that maybe in the process, I could find out a few things that might bring out the prince instead.

I was like most women: I'd heard that men were shallow and I believed it. I thought it would take two or three months at the most to learn everything that was worth knowing about this less-evolved gender. If someone had told me that studying men, and sharing

I was like most women: I'd heard that men were shallow and I believed it.

> **I thought how a man was with me was the kind of man he was.**

my discoveries, would become an obsession that spans two decades, I wouldn't have believed them. If someone had told me that I would become the world's biggest fan of men, I would have laughed hysterically. If someone had told me that unraveling the mystery of frog farming would help me unravel an even bigger mystery—how to keep and hold the true affection of men—I would not have slept nor eaten, nor let anything distract me.

I started with studying the men who were right in front of me. I was a business consultant for three single men at this time. I was their cheerleader, their confidante, their sounding board. We talked about everything in their lives. But as I worked with them, I had a new question… the question I was using to study men. The question was (and still is) this:

What if men are responding to women?

This is not an extraordinary question. We're responding to each other all the time, back and forth, back and forth, reacting to each other's words, facial expressions, body language, pauses, etc. I'm even responding to you the reader, to how I imagine that you are, as I write this.

My question was huge for me, because I realized that I didn't think that men were responding to me. I thought how a man was with me was the kind of man he was. So if a man was nice to me, I'd think, *Oh, what a nice man!* And I assumed he was nice 24/7. And if a man was a jerk to me, I'd think, *What a jerk!* And I assumed he was always a jerk.

It never occurred to me that maybe there was something that I'd said, or I'd done, or a look on my face, that he was responding to—until I started asking this question. Once I was open to it, I noticed that the same man would treat different women differently. The same guy would treat one woman like a barmaid, another like a sister and another like a princess. What had him do that? That was what I wanted to know. If he was the same guy—with the same history, upbringing and goals—what was it about her that inspired the different treatment? I especially wanted to know since I usually got the barmaid treatment.

> *What is significant about what I discovered is that they're the opposite of what we think!*

I left behind looking for who was to blame. I just wanted to understand how it all worked. I wanted to see the cause and effect so that wherever I was the cause, I could change my behavior and get a different result.

Starting with my three male clients, and expanding to men everywhere, I discovered numerous ways that men are responding to women. I have a long list of things— from insignificant to life-changing—that men do as a direct and immediate reaction to something that a woman did or said.

Surprisingly, I also learned an equally long list of ways

WHEN MEN ARE NOT RESPONDING TO WOMEN

My first book, Keys To The Kingdom, illustrates an important area in which men do not respond to women. This area is called the "Stages of Development" and describes the challenges and transitions encountered in the natural and unavoidable process by which a boy eventually becomes a fully-developed man. Unless they understand the Stages, women will likely experience tragic levels of unnecessary disappointment, pain and suffering. Mostly by taking men's stage-driven behavior personally.

On the other hand, if you think, *Oh, he's such a jerk!*, stop and consider, *Maybe I had something to do with it.* Once you think that, you might end up like me — wanting to know what you did that got you what you didn't want.

that men are not responding to women. Things that men do that they'd still do—no matter what a woman said, did or looked like—because it's part of being a man.

There are all sorts of ways that men are responding to women, and there are all sorts of ways that men are not responding to women. What is significant about what I discovered is that they're the opposite of what we think!

In other words, the things that we take personally, we shouldn't. The things that we don't take personally, we probably should. Really, if you get nothing else out of this book but to do the opposite of what you think you should do, you'll be more effective with men. Truly. No kidding.

Initially I set out to improve my romantic relationships.

... A revolutionary way of thinking about men and... the secrets to a lifetime of love, care and attention from all men.

Remember, I still had the dream. As it turned out, the same principles apply to all healthy men: fathers, brothers, male friends and co-workers, and men you encounter out and about.

In the pages that follow, I'll be sharing with you some of the most significant ways that men are responding to women. So that you can do something about the way men treat you. Through our workshops and seminars, thousands of women have used this information to have more satisfying relationships. These simple concepts reflect a revolutionary way of thinking about men and hold the secrets to a lifetime of love, care and attention from all men.

※ ※ ※

CHAPTER TWO

Men Are Not Hairy Women

Early on in my research, I had an insight into men that rocked my world. I kept watching and listening to the men I consulted, and when their behavior surprised me, I'd try to figure out their motivation. When I thought I understood it, I'd check with them. It didn't take long for me to come up dead wrong.

My client was talking to me about something he was supposed to do with his mother over the weekend. He didn't want to do it. So I coached him in ways that he could tell his mother that he wasn't going to do it, without hurting her feelings. I thought he was all set.

> *His answer was the beginning of a new life for me.*

When I talked to him the next Monday, I found out he'd done what his mother had asked. I thought, *He must have done it so his mom wouldn't be mad at him.* Then I asked him if that was true. His response shocked me. He said, "I would never do anything for that reason—and no self-respecting man would!"

But I thought it was a legitimate reason. Women do things all the time so someone won't be mad at us. But instead of getting defensive, I asked, "Well, then why did you do it?" His answer was the beginning of a new life for me.

He started telling me why he'd done it, and he was using words that were not in my daily vocabulary. I mean, I'd heard those words in movies from time to time. I'd read them in

> **Whoa! Are other men motivated by these things?**

books. But I'd never used them—and certainly not as a reason for why I'd done something. He used the words Duty, Obligation, and Honor. He talked about his duty as a son and fulfilling an obligation with his mother, and how it was a matter of honor that he did it—even when he didn't want to.

Whoa! I wondered, *Are other men motivated by these things?* Over the years, I've discovered that most men are. And as one man said, "And if they're not, you don't trust them."

This was my first eye-opener that the people I was studying were not a version of me.

I realized that as a woman, when I looked at a man, I didn't see a man. I saw a hairy woman. I interacted with him like he was a hairy, more muscular, uncouth woman. I expected him to know what every woman would know and do what every woman would do. I expected him to be motivated by the things I was motivated by. I expected him to use words the way that I use words.

> **Ninety-nine percent of the confusion and frustration between men and women is because we assume we're versions of each other.**

Ninety-nine percent of the

confusion and frustration between men and women is because we assume we're versions of each other. It goes both ways, although men are a little bit more forgiving. They allow for the mystery of women. But honestly, when men look at women they see a softer, more lovely, multitasking, emotionally-indulgent man. And they interact with us as if we're men!

Realizing that we're not versions of each other meant that I needed to pay much closer attention to men than I'd originally planned.

You know how men surprise you— and not in a good way? You know, when they do something that a woman would never do if she really cared about another person? When a man did something that I would never do, I thought, *What a jerk.* Or I'd think, *He's so selfish* or *He's so immature.* Or my very favorite one: *He's so unevolved!* Back when I started studying men, we didn't have the term "emotionally unavailable." I probably would have used it.

Back when I started studying men, we didn't have the term "emotionally unavailable." I probably would have used it.

This brings me to my second question:

What if there is a good reason for that?

After I'd come up with this question, whenever a man did something—one of those bad surprises—because I'm human, I still had the same reaction. I thought he was a

DIFFERENT REALITIES

Men are single-focused. They do one thing at a time. They commit themselves. "I'm going to get this done." This is why they get frustrated. They've committed themselves, and then they don't have everything they need.

When a man gets frustrated, we give him what would be excellent advice—if he was a hairy woman. We say, "Just do something else! If you can't fix the faucet, fix the fence! It's broken too!" He looks at us as if we're silly.

Women have diffuse awareness. Diffuse means "to pour in every direction." This is why we hear so many things in our environments talking to us, saying, "Pick me up! Fix me! Put me away! I'm ugly! Beautify me!" So we attempt to do eight to ten things at a time; pulled in every direction and committed to nothing.

Women don't get frustrated; we get overwhelmed. And then what do the men in our lives tell us to do? They tell us either to prioritize, or they say, "Just do one thing at a time." When they tell us that, we think, *That's stupid. If I did just one thing at a time, I'd be even more behind than I already am!*

We give each other advice from our different realities, from our different ways of thinking, because both men and women think that we're versions of each other. They're hairy, misbehaving women, and we're emotionally-indulgent men! These misperceptions are the source of most of our difficulties.

jerk or selfish or unevolved. And then I'd think to myself: *Wait a second, Alison. What if there's a good reason for that? What if he's not a jerk? What if he's not ridiculous? What if he's not stupid? What if he actually has a sound motivation for the thing he just did?*

So I started picking away at the new mysteries, asking the men around me: "Excuse me, would you mind explaining to me why you did that?" And then I'd put the imaginary duct tape over my mouth and just listen.

Men started to tell me their motivations. It was cute because they'd say, "Well, this is obvious, but I'll explain it anyway." Have you ever heard men use that word, "obvious"? We ask, "Why don't we talk about this?" And a man responds, "Well, because there's no point in stating the obvious." Men's behavior is completely obvious to other men. That's one of the reasons they use so few words!

Because I asked sincerely, and listened attentively, men started explaining themselves to me. And it was shocking. They explained this whole world where they're motivated by very different things than what motivates me—and most women, for that matter.

What is really exciting about their motivations, though, is that they are *good* things. They aren't bad things or bizarre things or perverse things. They are good things. They are wonderful things. I started to see how sensitive men are and that what they're sensitive to is good for women. It was neat. And it was really, really exciting.

What I learned about men changed my perceptions and changed me. My resentment washed away, my bitterness disappeared, my fear

What is really exciting about their motivations, though, is that they are good things.

I found out why the same man treats different women differently. And I found the answer to why men change after they catch us!

evaporated. I no longer felt I needed to punish men or be on guard against them. No surprise, then, that I soon met the love of my life.

Greg and I connected in September of 1991 and we were married in February of 1993. Living with Greg, I've had a lot of opportunities to ask my second question: *What if there is a good reason for that?* My son, meanwhile, was growing up, which provided even more opportunities for this question. Believe me; this way of thinking about behavior comes in handy with a teenager!

I'm still in contact with the men that I studied back then; and meanwhile, there have been hundreds of other men and hundreds of Panels of Men (see side bar) that I've been paying attention to with these two questions:

1. What if men are responding to women?
2. What if there's a good reason for that?

As a result of asking these two questions, I found out why the same man treats different women differently. And I found the answer to why men change after they catch us! The answers to both questions are ways that men are responding to women—and they do have *very good reasons for it!*

※ ※ ※

COULD IT REALLY WORK LIKE THIS?

At PAX Programs, we have four weekend workshops that are just for women where we show you, the participants, why men do what they do. Celebrating Men, Satisfying Women® covers all aspects of life, while Celebrating Men & Sex™ and Celebrating Men & Marriage™ focus on those particularly frustrating and confusing areas. Graduates describe the experience of our workshops as a series of light bulbs coming on. As we explain men to women, the women have insights and they gasp and laugh and cry and shake their heads in wonder.

But as the women are listening and learning, and it's making sense and it's illuminating and it's inspiring and hope is starting to grow, there's just this niggling doubt: *Could it really be this simple? Could it really work like this?*

At the end of the workshop, there is a panel of three or four real, live men. They're referred to us by graduates and other men who've had this extraordinary experience. As much as possible, we schedule men who are in different stages of their development (like Claudia explains in Keys to the Kingdom). They respond to questions that the workshop participants have submitted. And everything we've said throughout the weekend clicks. You hear it. You see it. You feel it. Then the doubt disappears and all the pieces come together.

CHAPTER THREE

Getting Men's Attention

✳

To make sense of men and their behavior with women, you have to understand how profoundly men are affected by attraction. The effects of attraction are lifelong. They determine the quality of the relationship from the first moment to the last—whether the last moment is thirty minutes or thirty years later.

You and I are told an awful lot about how to attract men. We're instructed mostly by television and magazine commercials. I was only a pre-teen when I already knew that it was the babe that looks the best in the bikini who gets the boys. So I worked really hard on that bikini body. Not so easy for a girl with the nickname "Chubbs."

Still, with all the input we get about being attractive, we remain baffled by seeing men pursue the not-so-perfect woman who appears to be playing hard-to-get. What is it about her?

So I worked really hard on that bikini body. Not so easy for a girl with the nickname "Chubbs."

The problem is that there are two completely different types of attraction, and we're only taught about one of them. First there's the type of attraction that gets attention from men. That's the one we know the most about. I grew up thinking if I got men's attention, it would lead to their affection. Right? But that is so not true! You can get a ton of attention, and zero affection— and be left painfully wondering what is wrong with you. The second type of attraction is what leads to your getting affection from men. This is the type we're told nothing about!

We don't know the limitations of sexual attraction and we don't know how to use it to our benefit at the right time.

I'm going to tell you about both types of attraction. You will understand the top 4 qualities that cause each type, and the 6 ways men respond when they're experiencing attraction. In other words, what does each type of attraction cause men to do? To keep is simple, here's a chart we'll fill in as we go.

Sexual Attraction		
CAUSE	④	①
	③	②
	②	③
	①	④
RESPONSE		

DO YOU KNOW THAT MEN ARE VISUAL?

If you're like almost all women, you know that men are disgustingly visual. Superficially visual. Visual and WRONG! After studying men since 1991, I now know that men are visual. Just visual. Well-designed visual. They're designed to acquire an enormous amount of information with their eyes. Why? Because it's efficient. It's a great way to collect information.

The first type of attraction we call "Sexual Attraction." Let's address this type of attraction that gets men's attention. Even though it's the one we know the most about, my research has revealed that we still don't know the most important things: We don't know the limitations of sexual attraction and we don't know how to use it to our benefit at the right time. Let's fix that.

Going in order from the least potent to the most potent, the four main causes of Sexual Attraction are:

#4: Shiny Hair

To understand how shiny hair causes Sexual Attraction, you have to go back a few years. About a million will do.

Now you know why there are so many commercials for shiny hair products—because shiny hair causes Sexual Attraction! The funniest thing about shiny hair, though, is that while it definitely causes Sexual Attraction—men don't know why! Do you?

To understand how shiny hair causes Sexual Attraction, you have to go back a few years. About a million will do. Think of our friend the Caveman. He had a predictable lifespan of maybe sixteen years; so he didn't have years or even months to get to know a woman. And he especially didn't have time to figure out the most important quality in a mate: If she was fertile. Which is what shiny hair could tell him.

If you're thinking that we've come a long way since cavemen, we haven't. The DNA of human beings has not changed at all in 10,000 years, and only slightly in the last 40,000 years.

What makes hair shiny is fat. Before Garnier Fructis and Pantene and all that stuff, shiny hair came from within. If a woman had enough fat in her diet and enough body fat, her hair would be shiny. And this was an indication that she was fertile. When women don't have enough body fat (at least 17%), we stop ovulating. It's nature's way of protecting us from starvation and from getting pregnant when we couldn't possibly carry a baby to term.

So shiny hair was a very efficient way to tell Caveman: "This woman's fertile. You should spend your resources on her. You should try to impregnate her!"

If you're thinking that we've come a long way since cavemen, we haven't. The DNA of human beings has not changed at all in 10,000 years, and only slightly in the last 40,000 years. We are still profoundly affected by the instincts passed down from our caveman and cavewoman ancestors.

WHAT IS IT ABOUT BOTTOMS?

We have a workshop called "Celebrating Men and Sex™," which includes a Panel of Men who have agreed to speak explicitly about sex. One of the questions a panel answered was: What is it about bottoms? They responded to the question for about ten minutes! They described all the different kinds of bottoms there are. They said, "Well, you know, there are firm bottoms and jiggley bottoms and wide bottoms and flat bottoms, and bottoms with more bottom on the top than on the bottom."

I'd never noticed there were so many kinds of bottoms. And I was wondering: *What kind of bottom do I have?* Because you never really know what it looks like back there, right?

Then the oldest of the men summed it up. He said: "What it comes down to is this: no matter the shape of your bottom, some guy is diggin' on it!"

You might be experiencing an instinctive reaction at this very moment... If you're worrying, *Oh my God, I don't have shiny hair.* I've had women come up to me and say, "People of my ethnicity never have shiny hair!" And the cavewoman within was panicking.

Do not worry about it. Seriously. We've asked hundreds of men, "What makes a woman attractive sexually?" As usual, a workshop panel of men had listed these things I'm about to tell you. And then one man said to the other, "Tell me the truth — What percentage of those things does a woman have to have for you to want to go to bed with her?" And the other man said sheepishly, "Five percent?"

So we've concluded you just need one shiny hair—or only five percent of the other three qualities I'm going to tell you about, because "shiny hair" is only the fourth most potent way to cause Sexual Attraction.

What's the third most potent way?

#3: Shapely Body

Sexual Attraction		
CAUSE	④ Shiny Hair	④
	❸ Shapely Body	❸
	❷	❷
	❶	❶
RESPONSE		

That's no surprise, right? Not to me either. What was a surprise to me, from listening to hundreds and hundreds of men, is that their definition of a shapely body is very different from mine. My ideal woman's body is about a size 2 and looks like a Barbie doll. Or like Scarlett O'Hara in *Gone with the Wind*, with her 17-inch waist.

Men have a much wider definition of a shapely body. They do, they really do. The way one man put it: "We don't call 'em hate handles!"

When we realize that men love all kinds of bodies, we can stop dating ass-backwards. What do I mean by that? What we normally do is see a guy we're attracted to and then go crazy trying to figure out how to get him. Right?

THE THIRD RESEARCH QUESTION

This is a question I come right out and ask men:

What is your favorite curve on a woman's body?

I recommend this question to you. Do a little of your own research and watch what happens. I'd start with a man you're not romantically involved with – so you have no attachment to the answer. After you ask the question, put the imaginary duct tape over your mouth and wait patiently. It'll be worth your while!

We contort ourselves into whatever we think he wants. We turn ourselves into a pretzel. If it seems like he's attracted to women with more makeup, we'll quick go put on more makeup. Or if he's attracted to girls without makeup, we'll quick go take some off. If it seems that he's attracted to the domestic ones, we'll try to act domestic. If it seems he likes the wild ones... and so on.

"We don't call 'em hate handles!"

All this is a lot of effort. Even when it works, it's hard to keep up. Some people might say it's lazy—but I'm not interested in more work, especially when less effort will get the job done. So this is what I would propose as a more energy and time efficient way to sexually attract a man and to keep his sexual interest and not have to work real hard at it: Catch the man who's already diggin' on your bottom! That's the guy to encourage. That's the guy who needs your smile. Because he likes the shape of your body as it is. And then what do you have to do to keep him interested in your body? Nothing! You don't have to lose any weight. You don't have to go to the gym. You don't have to do anything!

Some people might say it's lazy—but I'm not interested in more work, especially when less effort will get the job done.

It's obvious that the first two qualities, Shiny Hair and a Shapely Body, have to do with the way we look. But it's important to notice that they're number four and number three. The message we keep getting is that how we look is everything. But it's not everything. It's not even the best way to cause Sexual Attraction.

You could put a bag over your head and encase your body in tires, and the two most potent ways to cause sexual attraction would still work!

#2: Sensuality

Sexual Attraction			
CAUSE	❹ Shiny Hair	❶	
	❸ Shapely Body	❷	
	❷ Sensuality	❸	
	❶	❹	
RESPONSE			

Sensuality has nothing to do with what you look like. And—more than shiny hair, more than shapely bodies—sensuality causes Sexual Attraction. This is the good news and the bad news.

CAUSING A RUCKUS

You've probably figured out by now that I grew up with Barbie dolls. So, like many girls, I thought my body was supposed to look like Barbie's. Have you ever noticed that you could run a truck between Barbie's thighs?

I'm a very practical person. I think, out of a hundred women, there's maybe one woman whose thighs don't rub together. Right? And God bless her. But if you're just playing the odds, if 99 out of 100 women's thighs rub together, wouldn't that mean there's a pretty good chance our thighs are supposed to rub together?

In order to fully appreciate this way to cause a ruckus, you have to give up the idea that your thighs shouldn't rub together. And instead, explore: *If my thighs are supposed to rub together, hmm... maybe I could pay attention to them rubbing together...*

Try walking through a lobby, any lobby, and focus on what it feels like for your thighs. You might even walk with your knees closer together so you could feel more of your thighs rubbing. Ooh, that's even better. After you've focused on this pleasure for awhile, notice what has happened to the men in your vicinity. You'll see why I recommend a lobby—on the street, you'd cause an accident!

Sensuality is very simple to pull off. But it's one of the hardest things for women to do—because of "diffuse awareness." An estrogen-soaked brain is pulled in every direction. There are good reasons for this, but one consequence is that our attention is almost always divided. And sensuality comes from focusing on the pleasure your own senses are delivering to you. It could be a taste, a sound, a view, a smell or the feeling of something. In the moment that you are paying attention to that one pleasure, you are being sensual and it is a turn on to anyone watching you.

WHO TO BUY LINGERIE FOR

Have you ever tried to spice up your sex life with some lingerie? After listening to men, I figured out that when you buy lingerie, the trick is to buy the lingerie that turns you on. Buy the lingerie that causes you to go, "Whoa!" when you look in the mirror. Because if you're *feeling sexy,* you are *sexy.* And, if lingerie doesn't do it for you, wear what does. You can feel sexy in your sweat pants, and you can feel sexy in nothing!

Remember this the next time you want to seduce a man. Don't worry about the candlelight and music—that would seduce you and rarely works with them. Focus on completely receiving the pleasure of one of your senses. That will cause him to focus on the other pleasures he'd like to give you!

We've arrived. What's the number one quality that causes Sexual Attraction?

#1: Sexual Energy

Yep. Sexual ENERGY. You know what it is: It's the energy that a woman puts out when she wants to put out! The way men say it is: "What makes a woman sexy, is if she thinks she's sexy." And, "If a woman thinks she's sexy, she is!"

Sexual Attraction		
CAUSE	④ Shiny Hair	④
	❸ Shapely Body	❸
	❷ Sensuality	❷
	❶ Sexual Energy	❶
RESPONSE		

This means that the capacity to be sexually attractive is available to EVERY WOMAN. But, unfortunately, women don't pay enough attention to nurturing their sexual energy. We don't make it a priority because we haven't known how important it is. A little bit of attention in this area will give you a much higher benefit than thousands of dollars and hundreds of hours working on shiny hair and your ideal body.

One way to have more natural energy, and therefore sexual energy, is to SLEEP! Try to be exhausted and sexy at the same time. You can't. (Millions of mothers have tried, yes?)

This means that the capacity to be sexually attractive is available to EVERY WOMAN.

Our sexual energy and sensuality are forms of femininity—the nectar of the gods for men. Femininity requires real energy. We can be masculine on sugar, white flour and caffeine. We can be masculine on fumes, beyond exhaustion. But femininity requires real juice; it requires that our bodies be filled with Life Force. Learning what gives you the energy to be your

ADMIRATION FROM ONE VASE TO ANOTHER

Sexuality is entwined with the physical. When a man is strongly sexually attracted, he'll say he's "physically attracted." For decades, I thought that meant that he was attracted to a woman's body. NO! It means that the part of him that is attracted to her is his physical self. That is the part of him that is drawn to her. Not his spiritual, emotional or mental self.

The realm of the physical is made up of objects. This is why, when a man is very physically attracted, he'll express himself in appreciation of physical attributes. Like admiring a vase.

This is the source of comments that women find "objectifying." If a man makes comments about your body—in admiration or criticism—that make you feel diminished, that's a good indication that he's primarily sexually attracted and not experiencing the second kind of attraction.

When men make objectifying comments, our reaction is to think that he is a jerk. Maybe he's not. Causing high levels of sexual attraction is one of the best ways to bring out the worst in men. Stay tuned to find out how to bring out the best.

feminine self is one of the most important things you can do. If you doubt this, just ask a man.

Another way to nurture your sexual energy is to *climb back into your body!* When we find fault in our bodies, when they aren't good enough, when we're angry or sad about the way they are… we literally abandon our bodies. We don't like to think about them, look about them—heck, we don't even want to live in them! When

> **You will recover your own sexiness and you don't have to lose any weight to do it!**

we feel, think, and act that way, we lose access to our sexual energy, because that energy is inherently physical. So climb back in your body, move it around, take it out dancing. It's waiting. You will recover your own sexiness and you don't have to lose any weight to do it!

After you've learned to nurture your own sexual energy, then it's time to consciously use it. This means learning to turn it on and off at will, and directing it at the person you want to attract sexually. Some women who have high levels of sexual energy make the mistake of broadcasting it widely. This causes them to get "hit on" by lots of men, including plenty they'd rather not hear from! Unfortunately, they then blame the men—who are just responding to them! The trick is to direct your sexual energy like a laser beam at the lucky recipient. Just tickle him with it, not the whole room.

Sexual attraction is an enormously potent force in relationships. Being able to cause it when you want to—and to not cause it when you don't—is a skill every woman would do well to master. But, as important as sexual attraction is, it is tremendously LIMITED. Why? Because we expect sexual attraction to do more than it actually does.

How do men respond when they are sexually attracted? Sexual Attraction makes men want to have sex. That's it, honestly. Want to have sex period. The end.

Hundreds of men have confirmed it—all Sexual Attraction does is make a man want to have sex. It doesn't make him call back. It doesn't make him fall in love. It doesn't make him want a relationship. It doesn't make him want to spend money on you or spend a lifetime with you. It just makes him want to have sex. That's it.

Sexual Attraction		
CAUSE	❹ Shiny Hair	❶
	❸ Shapely Body	❷
	❷ Sensuality	❸
	❶ Sexual Energy	❹
RESPONSE	▶ Want to have sex .	
	▶	
	▶	
	▶	

The mistake we make is expecting more of Sexual Attraction than it actually generates. This is why we put too much of our time and resources into it. We're collectively spending billions of dollars on shiny hair, and billions of dollars and millions of hours trying to get our body to be the shape we think they want. All to get men—who think about sex up to every 57 seconds—to want to have sex! Am I wrong, or is that overkill?

About now you're probably getting interested in the other kind of attraction. Yes? Let's make sure we've got this one straight.

It doesn't make him fall in love.

Sexual Attraction is caused primarily by sexual energy, sensuality, shapely bodies and shiny hair. Easy to remember—the four S's. But before you memorize them, add the fifth "S" for *Silly* to pay too much attention to them. The real goodies with men are on the other side of the chart!

Before we look at the other type of attraction, there is something women must start paying attention to—for our happiness and our safety: High levels of sexual attraction cause men and women to experience something akin to hunger. And devouring the object of attraction seems like the best way to satiate that hunger. This puts men in "take mode" and women in "get mode."

When a man is in hungry, take mode, and relating to a woman as if she's a juicy meal, it gives women the heebie-jeebies. And rightly so, for he is much like his caveman ancestor at this moment. Our hair stands up on our necks and our instincts tell us to flee. Out of fear, we often react poorly and say something mean and emasculating, which serves to diminish and infuriate him. Not a smart thing to do to a caveman.

We'll put this man down—unless we are sexually attracted to him! Then our "get mode" has us go after him. We completely ignore our own intuition that is telling us this man is not focused on our highest good. Then we lie to ourselves that it could become something more than a sexual encounter. (Nothing against the purely sexual encounter. It's the faking ourselves out that worries me.)

When it turns out badly, we usually blame the man, thinking he was a jerk for only wanting sex and nothing more. But he was responding in exactly the same way that sexual attraction has caused men to respond for ages. On the other hand, sometimes we blame ourselves, wondering what is wrong with us that men don't want more from us. We're clueless that this scenario was entirely predictable because of the effects of sexual attraction on both genders.

It's Sexual Attraction that causes this mischief and heartache. It's hot, it's exciting, and it's got the monopoly on those surging hormones. But it's limited, it can be harmful, and the behavior chemistry causes can actually prevent the kind of attraction that gets a man's affection!

※ ※ ※

TAKING ADVANTAGE OF THE ADAM SANDLER EFFECT

When women find out how much chemistry works against us, they often wonder: *Is she saying I have to live without chemistry?*

The answer is "Yes... and no." If you insist upon the high levels of chemistry caused by an 8, 9 or 10 in your book, you will be doomed to being a ninny— disregarding your own intuition and good judgment, in a constant state of chemistry-driven horniness.

However, you don't have to go without physical attraction altogether. I recommend relying on the "Adam Sandler Effect." I discovered this while watching *The Wedding Singer.* I hadn't seen Adam Sandler before and I was shocked that this goofy-looking guy was a romantic leading man. But after awhile, I was charmed by his sweet nature and started thinking he was kind of cute. After even longer, I was mentally urging the Drew Barrymore character to kiss him, kiss him!

My own reaction to Adam Sandler inspired me to study the phenomenon of men growing on women, where we're not physically attracted and then one day, we think, "When did he get so handsome?"

This is fortunate. It means we can enjoy physical attraction without the intense stupidity that chemistry causes!

So why don't more women rely on it? Probably because the Adam Sandler Effect requires two things on a woman's part: 1) Giving up the concern of what others might think of you for being attracted to a man like that. Whether the prejudice is that he's short, chubby, bald, young, old, poor, badly dressed, etc.— whatever the characteristic that cavewoman-within and society-without would not choose for you. 2) Paying attention to what does attract you and ignoring the rest. If you don't like bald, quit looking at his head! This is a useful habit to build to nurture attraction in a long-term relationship because, as I like to say, *"Most men grow bald, many men grow fat and all men get saggy butts!"*

Stay tuned. The impetus for using the Adam Sandler Effect will grow as you learn about the type of attraction that gains more than men's physical interest...

CHAPTER FOUR

The Real Goodies

⁕

The second type of attraction is called "Charmed and Enchanted." Have you ever heard a man use those words? When a man is experiencing this type of attraction, he feels like he's under a magical spell. Men love feeling this way. It changes all of life. This is the type of attraction that gets affection from men.

Let's start with how men respond when they're Charmed and Enchanted. Then we'll show you what causes this potent form of attraction. Do yourself a favor and don't look ahead. It's more fun this way.

	Sexual Attraction	Charmed and Enchanted
CAUSE	❹ Shiny Hair	❶
	❸ Shapely Body	❷
	❷ Sensuality	❸
	❶ Sexual Energy	❹
RESPONSE	▶ Want to have sex.	▶ Spend time with
	▶	▶ Take care of
	▶	▶ Protect
	▶	▶ Contribute to
	▶	▶ Make happy

Look at the chart. Do these sound like the goodies to you? If a man *wanted* to do all those things for you, you wouldn't have to get him to, right?

It's actually even better than that. To be completely accurate, when a man is Charmed and Enchanted by a woman, he is *compelled* to do these things. He's compelled to spend time with you. He's compelled to take care of you. He's compelled to protect you. He's compelled to contribute to you. And he's compelled to make you happy. This means he's busy figuring out ways to do that and you don't have to figure out how to get him to. It's natural, it's effortless. It feels good for both sides.

Being Charming and Enchanting is the beginning of everything wonderful with men. It is the beginning of friendship, and a man's friendship should never be underrated. It's the beginning of romance and emotional involvement. It's the beginning of love and the beginning of devotion.

When a woman is Charming and Enchanting, she holds the key to a lifetime of love, care and attention from all men. But she needs to understand how it works.

At this moment, think about the men in your life. In your past and in your present. They might be members of your family, they might be friends, they might be men with whom you work. They might even be exes that just won't go away. Think of the men in your life who

It's the beginning of love and the beginning of devotion.

are trying to do these things—who are trying to spend time with you, trying to take care of you, trying to protect you, trying to contribute to you and trying to make you happy.

This one critical and significant thing about yourself—it could change your life...

Look around your workplace and your family and your friends and your old boyfriends. Can you see at least one man who's trying to do one of these? This is important because if you can see even one man who's trying to do these things, this tells you something significant about yourself. Something critical. And if you could remember this one critical and significant thing about yourself, it could change your life…

You are Charming and Enchanting.

Yes, you are charming and enchanting. Say it to yourself, *"I am charming and enchanting."* Go look in the mirror and tell the woman you see there, "You are charming and enchanting." Even if you don't believe it.

I know a young woman who spent a lot of time working on the left side of the chart, making sure she was sexually attractive. And, by our society's current standards, she had it: beautiful blonde shiny hair; a tall, athletic, model-shaped body; plus sensuality and sexuality. But her life had not turned out the way she'd hoped. Why weren't men falling at her feet?

Then she came to our "Making Sense of Men" seminar with her girlfriend. Every day for a week afterward, she called her friend on the phone and said, "I'm charming and enchanting! I'm charming and enchanting!" And she started walking around with a new attitude; the attitude of a woman who knows she's charming and enchanting. The attitude of a woman who knows she has what really matters. And since *men are responding to women*, it changed her whole life.

Put your hand on your heart, and say, "I am charming and enchanting." Do it until you feel it. Call a girlfriend and tell her, too.

You might recognize now that you are Charming and Enchanting to those men. But how do you become Charming and Enchanting for the men you want?

✳ ✳ ✳

WHEN MEN GENERATE ROMANCE

When a man is just Sexually Attracted, if he acts on it at all, it will be to generate a physical relationship. You can tell this is the case by what time he calls and what he invites you to do. Otherwise known as a "Booty Call."

When a man is just Charmed and Enchanted, he'll become a friend, mentor or big-brother figure. You cannot have too many of them. Treasure each of these men. They'll give you a lifetime of love, care and attention, too.

Available men generate romantic relationships with women for whom they experience both types of attraction.

CHAPTER FIVE

A Valuable Lesson in Men-glish

✳

When a man is Charmed and Enchanted, he doesn't say, "I'm Charmed and Enchanted by you; therefore, I'm compelled to spend time with you, take care of you, protect you, contribute to you and make you happy. Please let me." He doesn't say that. Here is a glossary so you can accurately interpret what men do say:

WORDS HE USES	WHAT HE'S SAYING	WHAT THIS MEANS
"Would you like some coffee?"	Can I spend time with you?	He's Charmed & Enchanted.
"Do you want to carpool?"	Can I spend time with you?	He's Charmed & Enchanted.
"Are you cold?"	Can I take care of you?	He's Charmed & Enchanted.
"Are you too warm?"	Can I take care of you?	He's Charmed & Enchanted.
"Are you hungry?"	Can I take care of you?	He's Charmed & Enchanted.
"I don't trust that guy."	Let me protect you.	He's Charmed & Enchanted.
"Buy a Volvo."	Let me protect you.	He's Charmed & Enchanted.
"Put your 401(k) in bonds."	Let me protect you.	He's Charmed & Enchanted.
"I could fix that for you."	Can I contribute to you?	He's Charmed & Enchanted.
"You should _____-"	Can I contribute to you?	He's Charmed & Enchanted.
"What do you like to do?"	Let me make you happy.	He's Charmed & Enchanted.
"What do you want for ___?"	Let me make you happy.	He's Charmed & Enchanted.
"Just tell me what you want."	Let me make you happy.	He's Charmed & Enchanted.

Are you getting the picture? In the future, when a man says any of these things to you, you want to hear: He's Charmed and Enchanted! He's Charmed and Enchanted. How delightful!

Except the odds are that you don't
find all these behaviors delightful.
Mostly we are annoyed when men
want to contribute to us. Mostly, we
don't know how to receive from

*It's a tragedy
because it could work
so beautifully...*

men. This is due to a host of misconceptions about
deserving and obligation, self-sufficiency and
independence. It's a tragedy because it could work so
beautifully if we would just let men be men.

When men are Charmed and Enchanted by us, they are
compelled to contribute to us. But we're often horrible.
We think they're actually insulting us. We interpret their
advice as, "You're too stupid to know this so I'm going to
tell you." That might be true with a woman, but not a
man. They're just Charmed and Enchanted, and they
need to contribute! You don't have to prove you're
smarter than he is. Men admire women's intelligence.
And they love that female intelligence gives women a
different and valuable perspective. So try a little
tenderness, okay? The next time a man gives you advice,

YOU'RE NOT HIS MOTHER

When a man says, "Are you cold? Here, take my jacket," a woman
will often respond, "But won't you be cold?" And then all the
chivalry goes right out the window—because it takes a man to be
chivalrous, and he just got treated like a five-year-old.

Men have asked me, "Why do women say that? Whether or not I'll
be cold is not the point!" And now you know – to him the point is
that he wants to take care of you.

DANGER! DANGER!

The more Charmed and Enchanted a man is by you, the more important it is to him to make you happy. He's got to make you happy.

If a man says to you, "You don't look happy," all your alarms should go off. The translation of this Men-glish is, *"This is torture. I don't know if I can make you happy, and if I can't make you happy, I have to go!"*

Think about it. Have you ever heard these words said on the way out? "You deserve someone who can make you happy." They're serious about it. Men leave women whom they can't make happy.

instead of shoving it back down his throat just think: *Charmed and Enchanted! Charmed and Enchanted— this is how he's showing he's Charmed and Enchanted!*

When a man is very Charmed and Enchanted, he doesn't say, "I'm very Charmed and Enchanted by you." He says something else, and it usually goes like this:

Say you've been dating for three months. That's when we want to know: *Where is this going?* We can play "getting to know you" for three months—but that's the limit. So we've promised our best girlfriend: "Tonight's the night. I'm going to ask the question. I'm going to find out where this is going."

Because we think we're dealing with a hairy woman, we think what will tell us where this is going are his feelings.

> **We can play "getting to know you" for three months–but that's the limit.**

We think his feelings will tell us the future—because, with a woman, they'd be the best indicator. Finally, we get up all our gumption and we ask, "How do you feel about me?"

Now he's really quiet, because the first thing he has to do is *find* his feelings. One of the things that men and women don't know about each other is that our feelings aren't even located in the same parts of our bodies! So he goes looking for his feelings.

Oh, my gosh, he realizes, *there's a big feeling here*. This is a difficult moment, because maybe he wasn't expecting a big feeling, and there it is! And then he'll have to decide whether or not he should tell you about the big feeling. Telling you about it will make him really vulnerable. He's just discovered he's emotionally involved, and when he tells you, you'll know that he's emotionally involved. He just found out he can get hurt here.

You'll know when he's decided to tell you because he'll give the man's international indication of commitment. This crosses all cultural boundaries. His shoulders will go slightly up and forward, and then back down. Like he's pushed his body into the future. This is what a man does when he's committed himself. Watch. Any time you see a man's shoulders move like that, you want to pay close attention to what he's about to say or do—because it's

> **He's just discovered he's emotionally involved.**

going to be important. He's committed himself to something.

So he found a big feeling. And he's committed himself to telling you about the big feeling. Then he says the big words: "I care about you."

IT MEANS MORE THAN LOVE

In one of our workshops, a woman responded to this information with an exasperated, "Why can't they just say 'I love you'?" A man replied, "Because it means more than that." This led to a spontaneous outpouring from several men of what "I care about you" meant to them. This is what three of them said:

- ▶ "It means you are the center of my world."
- ▶ "It means that everything I do, I do for you and our unborn children."
- ▶ "It means that I would do anything for you, including die for you."

He said it. He got it out. He told you about the big feeling. The future's opening up before him because he's told you about the big feeling—and he's glad of it.

He has no idea that over there, in your seat, you're thinking: *Oh, #%*$@! He 'cares' about me? Oh, no, not another one that just cares about me! That's the last thing I need, is another guy who cares about me! I care about my dog! I care about my car! I care about the person at the grocery store!*

> *I get so many mixed messages from women. I think we're really going somewhere. Then I tell her I care about her, and she breaks up with me.*

Oh, well…you thought it was really going somewhere. So you say, deep in resignation, "All right. Just take me home now, okay?"

Mystified, he asks, "What's wrong?" And thinking he must be really stupid, you say, "Nothing. Nothing's wrong."

Then the men come and tell me: "I get so many mixed messages from women. I think we're really going somewhere. Then I tell her I care about her, and she breaks up with me. Why is that?"

You know the answer! Because the same four words they use to tell us about the big feeling are the same four words we use to end a relationship!

"I care about you, but . . ."

The fifth word: BUT

"But… I'm just not attracted to you that way."

"But… I don't see this as going someplace."

"But… I don't think we have the same goals."

It's usually baloney after the "but." It just means "You don't do it for me." Or, "You don't have enough

> *Can you see the mismatch?*

money," "You're not handsome enough," etc. We actually don't really care about him. Which is why we are devastated when those words are said to us. Because we don't mean them when we say them, we don't pay attention to what they mean to men.

This is the beginning of being in love!

Can you see the mismatch? We're bummed when a man says, "I care about you," because we don't realize he just told us: "I'm emotionally involved here! I'm Charmed and Enchanted, and I find myself compelled to spend time with you and take care of you and protect you and contribute to you and make you happy—and this is the beginning of being in love!"

	Sexual Attraction	Charmed and Enchanted
CAUSE	❹ Shiny Hair	❶
	❸ Shapely Body	❷
	❷ Sensuality	❸
	❶ Sexual Energy	❹
RESPONSE	▶ Want to have sex.	▶ Spend time with
	▶	▶ Take care of
	▶	▶ Protect
	▶	▶ Contribute to
	▶	▶ Make happy
	▶	▶ Fall in love with

And that's what it comes down to—Charmed and Enchanted is the beginning of "in love." And it sounds

What else are we missing?

like coffee and jackets and carpooling and "I care about you."

If we're missing this communication, what else are we missing?

※ ※ ※

WHEN BUSY MEANS BUSY

Men are usually very direct and literal. If a man says, "I'm busy Saturday night," that means he's busy Saturday night. It doesn't mean he doesn't like you anymore or doesn't want to spend time with you or wants to break up. It just means he's busy. We think men send mixed messages because we try to interpret them as hairy women. This has us read more into their communication and not take it at face value.

The best way to understand what a man is saying is by looking it up in the dictionary. This is their book, really!

The Women's Dictionary would look like this: bus·y (biz ·i·) adj.

1. *If her back is to you, and she says it quietly, she's probably having hurt feelings and needs you to apologize.*

2. *If she says it emphatically, she's doing something you should be helping her with, but are not—as usual.*

3. *If the context is the future, her eyebrow is raised and her voice trails off, she's doing something she wants you to wonder about.*

CHAPTER SIX

The Goods that Attract the Goodies

✳

This is the moment some of us have been waiting for…What causes a man to be Charmed & Enchanted?

In speaking to and listening to thousands of men, I've found plenty of individual differences. And in the answers to many of my questions, I've found plenty of variations—but never in this area. I've asked hundreds of men about this and countless men have said, "Well, it's probably different for other men, but what I find incredibly attractive is _____" And then they all name the exact same quality.

The number-one quality that causes a man to be Charmed and Enchanted is:

#1: Self-Confidence

Self-confidence is the most attractive quality in a woman. It's irresistible. It knocks men over. It draws them in. It makes them feel like what they provide will really make a difference, because she's already fine. She doesn't need rescuing. They can relax. They can be themselves.

While self-confidence being the number one, far-and-away most attractive quality in women may seem like a breath of fresh air, it is actually not good news for women. Because each of us has an imaginary "friend" who rarely stops talking. She's that voice in our head that follows us around and tells us everything that's wrong with us. Her sentences start with "You're too...," or "You're not...," or "You should..."

Have you noticed that voice talks like it's a courtesy she's performing, pointing out your imperfections? Like she's doing you a huge favor? She talks like she's giving me great benefit by pointing out that I have a dimple in my butt. She points out that I should have dimples in my cheeks—but not in those cheeks. And she is so kind to elaborate by saying, "How could your husband possibly think you have the best butt in the whole world when you have a dimple in your butt? He must be lying about

ONLY FOR YOU

One of the most painful things for men is how much women don't like themselves. Because they adore us. They think we're amazing. They think we're beautiful. They're completely enchanted by our shapes and our smells and our mannerisms. And all those things that we would list as imperfections? To men, those are the things that make us who we are; that make us adorable and amazing and beautiful.

When I've talked to men about the ways a woman wants to change herself, the most common response is, "Well, if it will give her more confidence, then sure. But she shouldn't do it for me or for any man."

that. That must not be true. You should work on getting rid of that dimple in your butt."

It's confidence that makes men care about us, not perfection.

We call this voice "The Ideal Woman." This voice goes on about everything. Her aim is perfection. She is sure if you're perfect, you will live. Men will take care of you, women will like you, and you will survive. So it's compelling and urgent, correcting these imperfections. Yes?

Unfortunately, listening to the voice of the Ideal Woman kills our self-confidence. And she's missing the point— it's confidence that makes men care about us, not perfection. Part of being self-confident is being able to say to that voice: "Shut up! I'm good enough. I like me."

Women are usually what I call "Externally Motivated." Besides our environments goading us into task after task, we're highly susceptible to other people's opinions. It is the opposite of men, who are generally "Internally Motivated." That means that everything men do is because they are internally compelled or inspired to do it. They don't respond to external influences the way women normally do and are not affected the same way by criticism (see page 54).

Being Externally Motivated is our greatest weakness— and the source of our wisdom and magic. It is the source of the feminine essence which is absolutely irresistible and necessary to men. But it makes self-confidence harder to attain and maintain.

> *Whatever it is, don't feel silly or guilty about providing it for yourself.*

To solve this problem, I started paying attention to "Confidence," in addition to "Self-Confidence." It's not as potent but it will do in a pinch. Confidence is something you can easily give yourself by working with your external orientation—instead of making yourself wrong for it. I may not always have self-confidence (see box), but I can boost my confidence from a variety of ways by understanding how I tick. For me, it can be as simple as wearing the right shoes. It may seem silly, but it's true. If I have shoes that tickle me, that please me, that go with my outfit (whether it's sweatpants or pearls)—I am unstoppable.

Find out what gives you confidence and do it everyday. Is it shoes or purses? Manicured nails or a great hair cut? It could be feeling healthy from eating good food. Or feeling fit from taking your body out for a spin. Whatever it is, don't feel silly or guilty about providing it for yourself. Ultimately, your being confident contributes to everyone.

So what's the number-two quality that causes a man to be Charmed and Enchanted?

#2: Authenticity

One of the highest compliments a man can pay a woman is to say that she is "real." They see it as being courageous—a woman who has the courage to just put herself out there and be who she really is.

Can you see that authenticity would go with self-confidence? That the more confidence you have, the more authentic you'll be able to be? The more you like yourself, the more you'll be able to be yourself.

Men have what they call a "BS meter." It's factory-installed equipment in a man. They can tell a fake very easily and they hate all forms of inauthenticity in women, including manipulation and strategy. Men love it when we're direct and authentic. This is why the men we're hot for—the men we contort for—rarely like us!

You might be seeing now that what makes us Charming and Enchanting to men is also good for us. It's a win-win situation.

WHAT IF I'M NOT SELF-CONFIDENT ALL THE TIME?

Are you worried that when you're not self-confident, he's going to stop being Charmed and Enchanted? Thankfully, since authenticity is the second most Charming and Enchanting quality, you can be authentic about your temporary lack of self-confidence!

Just be straight-forward and honest and say something like, "I'm not feeling very self-confident right now. Could you tell me you like my butt even though it has a dimple in it?"

I said that to my husband, Greg, once, and he said, "What dimple?"

This is classic MAN and I love it. The combination of being Single Focused and nurtured by beauty. So their eye is drawn to beauty while single focus naturally screens out everything else.

(Either way we win—there are some men who love all dimples and would be diggin' on that!)

CONFIDENCE AND CHEMISTRY ARE NOT GOOD BED FELLOWS

The experience of "chemistry" is literally your body's hormonal reaction to a potential mate. It reacts to the characteristics that your cavewoman-within perceives as ideal to protect you and provide for you and to make great babies for the future of our species. This is why height, strength, resources, status and beauty cause such strong reactions in us. It's also why we're attracted to men of integrity and intelligence; two qualities that are perceived as strengths.

The cavewoman-within expresses her approval by flooding our bodies with "chemistry." This puts women into Get Mode and we immediately start adapting to that man.

When you're experiencing strong chemistry, are you experiencing self-confidence? Are you being authentic? Or are you adapting your personality and preferences to what you think he wants?

The message is this: When we are under the influence of chemistry, we become the OPPOSITE of Charming and Enchanting. This is why the men we want don't like us. Because they've never even MET us! They just experience the twisted up pretzel version of ourselves that chemistry produces every time.

What to do? RUN from the chemistry and take advantage of the Adam Sandler Effect. Give one of those men, who's in love with the real you, a chance to win your heart and your body!

So what's the number-three quality that causes a man to be Charmed and Enchanted?

#3: Passion

What are you passionate about? Your career? Your volunteer work? Salsa dancing? Scrabble? Expressing your passions is really, really, really, really important— especially if you like men to listen to you. When a woman talks about her passions, scientists have actually been able to measure an increase of a well-being hormone in a man's body. She expresses her passions, and he's flooded with a sense of well-being.

	Sexual Attraction	Charmed and Enchanted
CAUSE	❹ Shiny Hair	❶ Self-Confidence
	❸ Shapely Body	❷ Authenticity
	❷ Sensuality	❸ Passion
	❶ Sexual Energy	❹
RESPONSE	▶ Want to have sex.	▶ Spend time with
	▶	▶ Take care of
	▶	▶ Protect
	▶	▶ Contribute to
	▶	▶ Make happy
	▶	▶ Fall in love with

I've studied men since 1991 the organic way—by watching them and listening to them in daily life. But now scientific studies are backing-up my discoveries. It's awesome. One way is with magnetic resonance imaging

WHY WOMEN CRITICIZE MEN

Because women are generally externally motivated, the easiest way to change a woman is to criticize her or complain. It can even be a comment someone casually tossed off, like, "Hmm, that color's not good on you." She'll adapt without even having to think about it.

This is why women criticize men. Since to us they are just hairy women, we think what changes us will change them: "You don't bring me flowers anymore!" If you said that to a woman, she'd bring you flowers. She would resent it, but she would bring you flowers!

We're shocked that men don't spring into action when we criticize them. We think it means they don't love us or respect us. But that's not true. He does love you. He does respect you. But criticism won't change him. It'll just drive him away from you.

Does this mean you can't change a man's behavior? No. You absolutely can change his behavior. You just need the right Men-glish and the right attitude.

(MRI) being used on the brain. For years, I've talked about the effects of women's complaining on men. How it kills men's energy. How it's so life-sucking that they have to get away from it. Recently scientists have used MRIs to see that women's voices are processed in the same part of men's brains that processes music. Music! Then, can you imagine what complaining sounds like?

Can you imagine what complaining sounds like?

Once again, the Charming & Enchanting qualities go together. The more self-confident you are, the more authentic you can be; the more authentic you can be, the more you can express your passion. When we don't have self-confidence, our passions go underground. We stop talking about them. We stop expressing them.

By the way, don't worry what you're passionate about. It could be ending world hunger or baking the perfect chocolate chip cookie. It's expressing the passion that matters.

FINDING YOUR SELF

Women can find anything. This goes way back to women specializing in the gathering half of hunter-gatherers, while the men specialized in the hunting half. With our Gatherer's Vision, we can scan a room and locate an object quickly. With our Gatherer's Data Base, we've often already noted an object out of place.

But finding our selves is the hardest thing. As the Master Adapters of our species—truly our strength—we can easily misplace ourselves while unconsciously adapting to the needs and values of a relationship, a family, an organization, even a society.

In our Celebrating Women: Regarding Ecstasy & Power™ workshop, we guide women through a process to find themselves. Each participant articulates the true, eternal essence of her being. Once she's accomplished this, we teach her how to set up her life to nurture her true self—so that her daily routines nurture her essence instead of rob her of it.

When you have identified your SELF, then you have access to true Self-Confidence. Meanwhile, don't be afraid to invest in some great shoes.

You might now be thinking: *I'm confident. I'm authentic. I'm passionate. So why isn't it turning out? If I've got the top three things, why am I not getting all the goodies?* Or you might be thinking: *They start out doing all that stuff, but it doesn't last!*

So close, yet so far. The problem is number four. The fourth quality is where it goes awry. We have the confidence, we have the authenticity, we have the passion, and we draw men to us. That's what attraction means, to draw to oneself. We draw men to us, but we don't have the fourth quality—and it sends them packing! It's over. They have to go. And we don't understand why.

What is the fourth quality that causes a man to be Charmed and Enchanted? I saved the fat pen for this one!

	Sexual Attraction	Charmed and Enchanted
CAUSE	❹ Shiny Hair	❶ Self-Confidence
	❸ Shapely Body	❷ Authenticity
	❷ Sensuality	❸ Passion
	❶ Sexual Energy	❹ **Receptivity**
RESPONSE	▶ Want to have sex.	▶ Spend time with
	▶	▶ Take care of
	▶	▶ Protect
	▶	▶ Contribute to
	▶	▶ Make happy
	▶	▶ Fall in love with

#4: Receptivity

What is Receptivity and why is it so important? There are two kinds of receptivity that men need—and they can't live without either of them.

The first kind of receptivity men need is women being open and responsive to all the ways they express caring for us. Allowing their unique expressions of that big feeling in how they take care of us, protect us, contribute to us and make us happy. These are gifts they offer, and they need us to be receptive to them. (Does this mean you never have boundaries? No! But we need to learn to express them graciously as well.)

He puts his heart into it. And he needs something back.

Men can't change that they need this kind of receptivity from women. When a man is Charmed and Enchanted it puts him in a different mode, the one I call "Give Mode." You can relate to this if you think about it, because you and I get Charmed and Enchanted by children, by girlfriends, by men, by people we just met. And, just like men, when we're Charmed and Enchanted, we want to give to that person. We are naturally thinking of and looking for things we could do for them.

Combine Charmed and Enchanted together with Single Focus, and you've got a man who's putting a lot of effort into figuring out, *What can I do for her?* He's very intense about that question. He spends time and energy and resources. He puts his heart into it. And he needs something back: he needs the energy that flows back to him when his gifts are well received.

Unfortunately, over the last 30 years, you and I have been taught to value ourselves for masculine characteristics. We've been taught to think that the value of a woman is in how productive she is, how generative she is, how much she can make happen, how much she controls, how much she manages. These are masculine values.

We spend much of our time proving we don't need anybody. Proving we can do it all ourselves. So when a man is in Give Mode, we're stuck in: *No, I don't need that. No, I don't deserve that. No, I've already got one of*

NOT WHAT THEY EXPECT

Thousands of thousands of years ago, women traded sex for food. It's ancient—trading sex for food—and it's still in our instincts. This is why we're afraid if a man buys us dinner, he's going to expect sex. Therefore, we won't let him buy us dinner.

There are very few men who expect to get sex that easily (which doesn't mean they're not hoping). But because we don't always have that self-confidence, and we don't know why men love women in the first place, we don't know that for them it's a pleasure to get to spend time with us and to contribute to us.

One of the things men like to give women is a nice meal. All they need in return is that we receive it graciously. Unfortunately, this common misunderstanding prevents receptivity as early as the first date.

those. No, I can buy that for myself. No, you really shouldn't spend that money.

We'll also do a whole avoid-the-payback thing: *I don't deserve this.* We're really saying, *I don't feel I've earned it yet, and I don't want to owe you—especially in the currency I think you're going to want to collect.*

All this adds up to our not being receptive to their gifts, to their masculine expressions of their enchantment. In frustration, they have to go away.

The second kind of receptivity men need is even harder for contemporary women to provide. We've actually been taught that it would be wrong to give it. It would be a betrayal of the sisterhood.

We spend much of our time proving we don't need anybody.

Men need us to be receptive to who they are. The way one man said it was, "There's nothing like looking in a woman's eyes and seeing that she accepts you."

We've been taught to NOT accept men. Our culture has the attitude that you're selling out if you accept men. We're not supposed to "put up with" their being men. After all, they're just hairy, misbehaving women who ought to know better. Don't accept them, punish them! The fear is that we have to put in the discipline, or they'll just get worse. But it's just because we don't understand them.

| **"Man Magnets."** | The more you learn about men and their world and why they do what they do, the more naturally |

receptive you'll be to them. Because who men really are is SUCH GREAT NEWS! You won't have to try to be receptive to them; you just will be, effortlessly. And as you find out how willing and able they are to give you what you need most, you'll relax and be able to accept them.

This receptivity to who men are is incredibly Charming and Enchanting and one of the reasons why some men call the graduates of our Celebrating Men, Satisfying Women® workshop, "Man Magnets."

✳ ✳ ✳

SUPERFICIAL? NO! SUPER-PERCEPTIVE!

Many women complain that men judge them by their looks. We assume that this is men being superficially visual. Not so! Unbeknownst to most women, men can perceive the qualities of self-confidence, authenticity, passion and receptivity in a woman—JUST BY LOOKING AT HER!

Her confidence shows in the way she carries and moves her body. Authenticity is expressed in how comfortable she appears in her body and clothes, and in the easy directness of her gaze. Passion lights up her eyes, cheeks and smile. Receptivity is obvious from the softness of her eyes, mouth and jaw, and in open arms and a relaxed posture. When a woman is not receptive, men often describe her face as "edgy."

For my husband, Greg, it was love-at-first-sight. I didn't understand how that was possible in any meaningful way until I fully comprehended the effects of attraction and how super-perceptive men are. All these years later, he wakes up each morning and rejoices that I am there beside him. He reaches out to snuggle with me and is greeted with a contented purr. He's always moved by that simple receptivity. Which goes to show you – you can even Charm and Enchant a man while you're sleeping!

CHAPTER SEVEN

Down the Toilet or Up the Spiral

✳

This is going to explain a lot of life. Unfortunately, it's not the pretty part of life. But it could put you on the path of a lifetime of ecstatic moments with men. Because the effects of attraction are lifelong, while you have confidence, authenticity, passion and receptivity, men will be compelled to give you all the goodies… the love, care and attention you crave.

You give them the wood – they give you the fire.

It's simple cause and effect. It's like wood and fire. You give them the wood—they give you the fire. Now, if you hear that in a sexual connotation and it helps you remember it, that's fine. Whatever it takes to have you remember that, in this case, men are responding to you!

What happens if you stop putting wood on the fire? It dies. And this is what happens in our relationships. We don't take care of our self-confidence, or shoe-confidence, and moments later the authenticity and the passion and the receptivity go out the window. It doesn't take long for men to stop being charmed and enchanted. In fact, it's immediate!

It usually works like this:

✳ You start out in a new relationship. You just met, you really hit it off and it's so exciting.

✳ You're thinking: *Where have you been all my life? This is so much easier than my other relationships! This is great! You're wonderful, I'm wonderful. You're so generous with me. You want to spend all this time with me. I don't have to come chasing after you. You're always calling me and generating it with me. I feel like I'm in a movie! This is fabulous!*

✳ Then he does something. They always do something. Right? They're late. They don't call for two days. They look at another woman. They don't give you what you need. (It could be that he gave up because you weren't receptive.)

✳ He does that something that has you think, *I would never do something like that to someone I really cared about!*

✳ When he does that something, being a woman, you have a question: *Why? Why? Why did he do that?*

✳ And because you're a woman, you will always answer the question! You'll answer the question from your frame of reference. And the answer

He did that because he doesn't care about me...

will be some version of: *He did that because he doesn't care about me or love me or respect me enough to not have done that.*

* That's what you'll conclude… because if you cared about a person or respected a person or loved a person, you would never have done that. Therefore, he must not love, respect or care about you enough. And you figure out a combination of those three depending on the circumstances.

* But because you're a woman, once you've concluded that he doesn't love you or respect you or care about you enough to not have done that, you have a question.

* What's the question?

* *Why? Why doesn't he love me enough or care about me enough or respect me enough?*

* And, because you're a woman, the voice of the Ideal Woman will answer that question for you. She'll tell you what is wrong with you. She'll tell you what you are too much of, or too little of, that has him not love you enough.

* In that moment, your self-confidence takes a big hit and you start trying to change yourself.

✳ You're now less self-confident and less authentic, and you're too busy trying to improve yourself so your passions go unexpressed…

Immediately, he is no longer compelled to spend time with you...

✳ All of which he responds to by being less Charmed and Enchanted.

✳ And, immediately, he is no longer compelled to spend time with you and take care of you and make you happy…

✳ You notice he doesn't call as much or generate as much, but not knowing the true source, you wonder, *Why?*

✳ And it starts all over again; you losing self-confidence, him losing attraction, with a little complaining or criticizing thrown in for seasoning.

✳ And it keeps going, down, down, down…

✳ Until this magnificent, confident, authentic, passionate woman turns into a sniveling, whiney, why-don't-you-call-me-as-often nag.

This is what we call the Toilet. And how it gets flushed—the beginning of the downward spiral—is the expectation we have that men behave like women. It's not his action that hurts our self-

This is what we call the Toilet.

confidence. It's what we think it means. And our reference is women!

Men ask me, "Why do women change? They're so amazing in the beginning and then they change. Why do they always change?"

Do you remember a complaint like this from the beginning of the book? This is where it all comes together. It's true—men do change when they catch us. *Because we change! And, in this way, men ARE responding to women.*

We change when we're caught. We get attached, and now we take everything personally. We think everything a man does means something about us. Then we lose self-confidence, we stop being authentic and we stop expressing our passion. We stop being receptive and start grasping. We start taking as much as we can, because we've got this empty space inside us, where our self-confidence used to be, that we're trying to fill from them.

We change and they respond to us. They are charmed and enchanted until we stop being charming and enchanting. This might take three months. It might take three years. It might take 30 years. It doesn't matter how long it takes. It has the exact same effect.

1. When we stop taking care of our self-confidence, men stop being compelled to take care of us.

2. When we stop being ourselves, men can't find us to love us.

3. When we stop sharing our passions, we stop inspiring their passion.

4. When we stop being receptive to men, they have to stop giving to us.

> **You can cause a lifetime of love, care and attention from all men.**

You can cause a lifetime of love, care and attention from all men. The opposite of the Toilet is the Upward Spiral. This happens when you notice the men who are Charmed & Enchanted by you and then consciously set them up to succeed. Since he is in Give Mode, he needs to know what you need and what makes you happy. Tell him, preferably using Menglish. Then relax and appreciate his efforts and results.

Your gracious receiving will fuel him to even greater efforts. And for this, he'll need even more information, because he's not a hairy woman and he's not a mind reader! As you consistently provide the information he needs and the receptivity he thrives on, the spiral will go up and up and up. This is the real happily ever after.

Can you see how it's in your hands? What will you do now?

Congratulations for having the courage and curiosity to Make Sense of Men. Let the adventure continue!

✳ ✳ ✳

Related Products and Programs
from
PAX Programs Incorporated

The Celebrating Men, Satisfying Women®
workshop series:

Celebrating Men, Satisfying Women®

✳ Learn why men do what they do—so you know when to
take something personally and when to not!

✳ Learn how to tell men what you need, without criticism
or complaint, so they act upon your needs instead of keep
their distance.

✳ Learn Men-glish and end the mixed messages you send
and receive.

✳ Stop Frog Farming and bring out the best in men

✳ Be more confident in the knowledge of what men love
about women

Celebrating Women: Regarding Ecstasy & Power™ (aka The Queen Workshop)

❋ Articulate your essence, learn how to nurture your self-confidence and fill your other feminine needs.

❋ Practice receiving and practice setting boundaries; they are two sides of the same phenomenon and essential to healthy relationships.

❋ Find out what makes a woman worth dying for

Celebrating Men & Sex™

❋ Learn the surprising things men value and what they need from sex.

❋ See how emotional and intimate men want to be.

❋ Learn how to honor your needs and be more self-expressed and satisfied.

❋ Experience a new freedom to communicate about sex with your partner.

Celebrating Men & Marriage™

❋ Learn how to use problems to strengthen your relationship.

❋ Learn how to tell if a man can fulfill your needs without months of investing your time and energy.

❋ Learn how men approach serious relationships versus casual dating, and what qualifies a woman for marriage.

Products on CD and DVD

Understanding Women: Unlock the Mystery
Workshop-to-Go on DVD

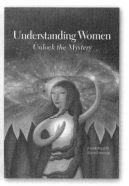

After more than a decade of helping women to understand men, PAX Programs has unraveled the complexities of women.

❊ Be surprised by the reason women are compelled to multi-task

❊ Note which conversational details need remembering and which don't

❊ Discover the true source of women's jealousy and competitive behavior

❊ Learn to repair hurt feelings and save you both from the "Rage Monster"

In Sync with the Opposite Sex
Workshop-to-Go on CD

❊ Unravel the mixed messages you receive.

❊ Avoid coming on too strong.

❊ Eliminate the pitfalls in pursuing the one you want.

❊ Learn the benchmarks and timelines of dating and relationships, so you don't blow it.

Contact Information

PAX Programs Incorporated
Understandmen.com
(800) 418-9924
P.O. Box 56749
Sherman Oaks, CA 91413

Author's Note

✳

My study of men began with taking responsibility for my part in the quality of our interactions and relationships. I believe both men and women are most successful with each other when we look to ourselves first. As you work with the material I have provided here, I hope that you'll apply the "where the shoe fits, wear it" rule to have the biggest impact on your relationships with the opposite sex.

Occasionally, a man does not respond the way I've described in this book. When that happens, I recommend first examining whether or not you are emasculating him in any way. Even ask him. Then do a check up on yourself — are you being self-confident, authentic, passionate and receptive? Are you providing the information he needs, in a language he resonates with (Men-glish), at a time that is actionable? Are you providing loads of appreciation?

If you've tried everything, consider that he may not be responding to you. Sometimes men have been so negatively affected by women in their past, that they are not willing to be charmed and enchanted by any woman. In this case, his actions won't follow the pattern I've described and, if you feel diminished by him in any way, it would be wise to avoid him.

✳ ✳ ✳

About the Author

※

Alison Armstrong lives in southern California and western Colorado with her husband, Greg, and their two daughters. In addition to sharing her knowledge of men and women through books and recorded programs, she teaches workshops regularly at PAX Programs Incorporated. She is the founder of LOVE Africa, Inc., a non-profit ministry which receives a portion of the sale of this book.

※ ※ ※

Notes

Notes

Notes

Notes